Dave Berg
Looks At The
NEIGHBORHOOD

D1570285

WARNER BOOKS

A Warner Communications Company

KIDS
IN THE NEIGHBORHOOD
.....WHERE CHILDREN SHOULD BE SEEN BUT NOT HURT.

HIDE AND GO PEEK

7

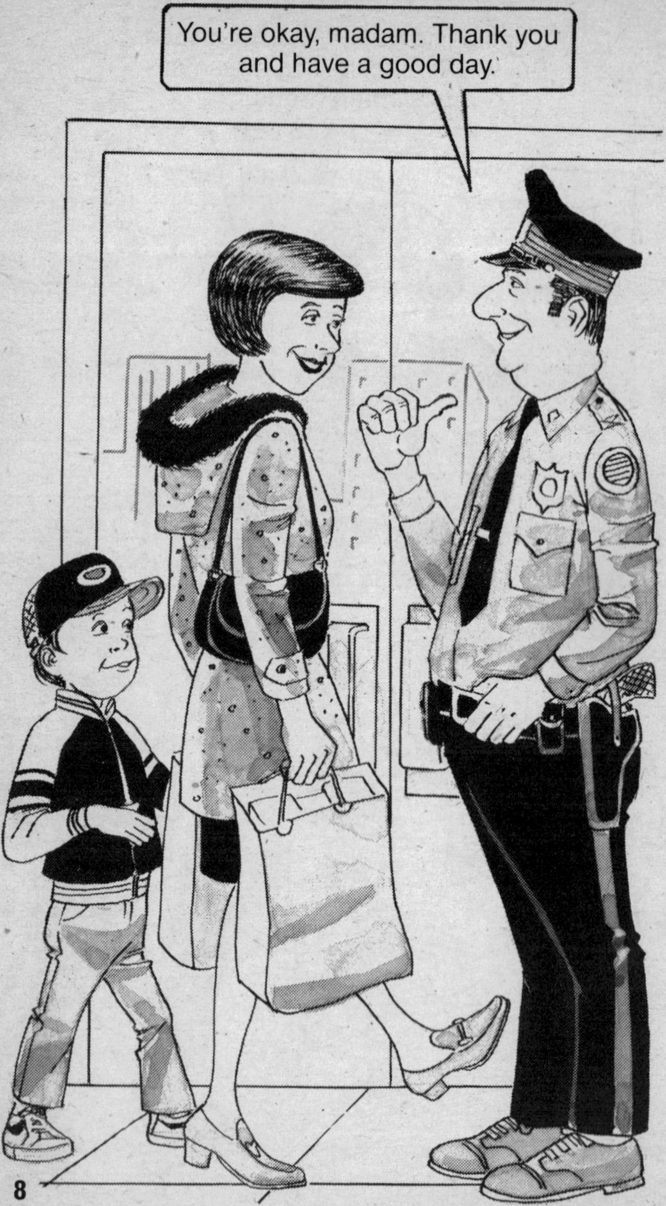
You're okay, madam. Thank you and have a good day.

9

LITTLE BOY BLEW

THE MOVING FINGER RIGHTS

13

READING AND RIGHTING

FORGETTING TO REMEMBER

16

SEE SAW

19

FIXMASTER

20

21

PLAY IT BY YEAR

22

23

SHAPE OF THINGS TO COME

24

25

FLEE SPEECH

27

STARTING OFF WRITE

29

33

SPEAK QUEASY

34

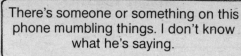

③

④

35

SHARE COPPERS

NOURISH-MEANT

41

SON BURNT

42

43

SHIRKAHOLIC

①

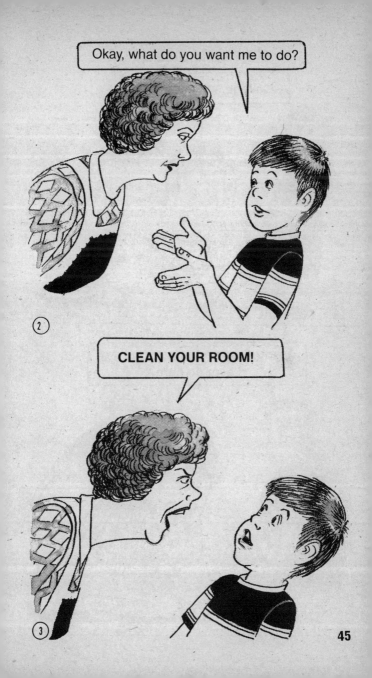

45

SOME COME LOUDER

CRIME DOESN'T PREY

My God! The crime rate is going up again.

We've got to find a way how to **stop** all this **law breaking.**

48

49

51

53

SPLITTING HEIRS

55

56

SPORTS
IN THE NEIGHBORHOOD

**WHERE THE ONLY ONES WHO ARE HAPPY ABOUT
BEING OVER THE HILL ARE THE JOGGERS.**

THE HIGH AND THE FLIGHTY

A SIGHT FOR SORE GUYS

61

HIGH WIDE AND HADSOME

WOW! Look how big those basketball players from the east coast are. They must be **seven feet tall.**

I know.

I wonder what they do when they're not playing a game.

Every Saturday they fly out here to this town. Then they drive down to the local movie theater.

③

Then they deliberately **sit down in front of me** every time.

④

63

THE HIGH AND THE ALMIGHTY

Grandpa, kite flying has changed greatly since you were a kid. There are all kinds of brand new shapes, like airplanes, and flocks of birds and giant pollywogs with long long tails.

And the materials they are made of are brand new kinds of plastics and other new fabrics.

65

SEE WORTHY

67

RUNNING BORED

GOING DOWN IN DEFEAT

I'll be darned! Roger Kaputnik, who is always laughing at **joggers** is now **jogging himself.**

Hey, Roger, I didn't know you were into jogging.

I'm not.

FOR WHOM THE BELLS TALLS

JOGGING A MEMORY

① ②

ACTION PACT

GAMESMANSLIP

83

DAZE ARE NUMBERED

85

86

THERE'S COLD IN THEM THAR HILLS

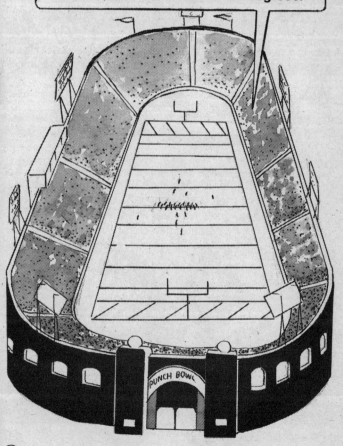

NEIGHBORS
IN THE NEIGHBORHOOD

.... WHERE EVERYBODY MINDS YOUR OWN
BUSINESS.

THE PRICE IS BRIGHT

SEASONED GREETINGS

With today's economics we were having a hard time making ends meet.

So to lick it we took out a loan and bought an economy car.

But that means you'll have to pay ridiculously high interest rates to the bank.

93

COLOR BLINDED

95

A SPOUSE DIVIDED

Right! The way we used to, I'll **wash**....

③

.....and you **break**!

④

101

MONEY BALKS

FATHER SHOWS BEST

> I must say, my husband is a very good and attentive father to the children.

> Every night, right after supper, no matter how tired he is, he sits down and does something with the kids.

THE SON ALSO RISES

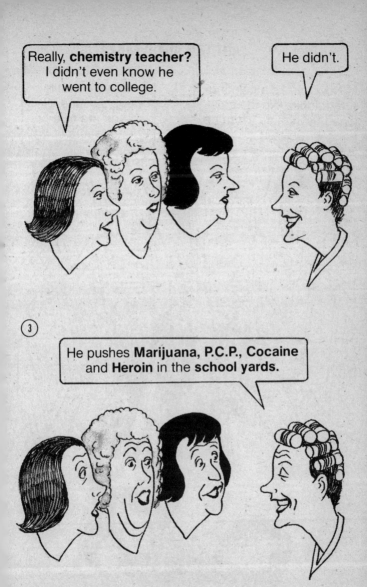

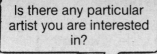

Is there any particular artist you are interested in?

Oh yes, most definitely.

(2)

Any artist that painted a picture that will **fill an empty space** exactly **twenty four** and **three quarter inches** by **thirty eight** and a **half** inches.

(3)

111

113

DRINK TO ME ONLY WITH THINE BUYS

114

115

TEACHING A NEW DOG OLD TRICKS

Ha! Some trained dog. You say **"sit!"** and he **jumps.**

(3)

(4)

AMERICAN TELL AND TELL

121

TRIPS THAT PASS IN THE NIGHT

123

SMOKE GETS IN YOUR GUISE

125

PLANE FACTS

126

Of course you're scared. It's perfectly normal. **I'm** scared too. **Everybody** in the plane is scared.

③

Even the **pilot** is terrified.

④

GETTING THERE IS HALF THE FUND

Because if He did, He **also** wouldn't have made it so **darn** hard **to get to the airport.**

SEATING IS BELIEVING

WELL WISHING

132

This is the most **pleasant** store I ever shopped in. All the employees are so **polite**.

134

MORALE
IN THE **NEIGHBORHOOD**

...WHERE TO SOME PEOPLE, EVERY DAY IS ONE
OF THOSE DAYS.

137

ILL GOTTEN BRAINS

141

TOO SIDED

THE BEGGAR THEY ARE THE HARDER THEY FALL

145

EXPRESS-SHUN

I spent all day cooking everything you like. So do you show any appreciation? **No!**

Do you say, **"Mom, this is a delicious meal."**? **NO!** Do you say, **"Thank you, Mom, for slaving over a hot stove making me a scrumptious meal!"**? **NO! You just sit there stuffing your face.** So **say** something already.

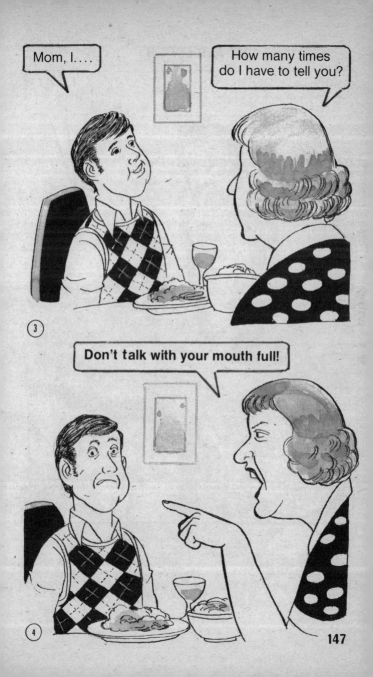

147

LIB AND LET LIB

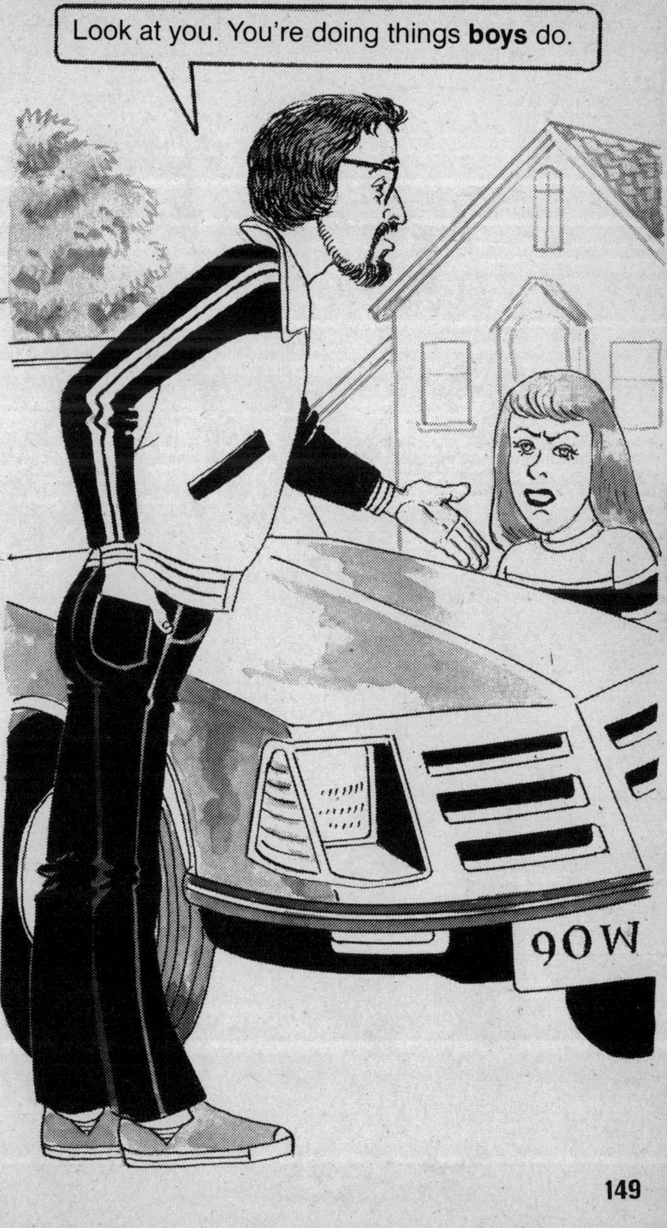
Look at you. You're doing things **boys** do.
90 W

151

NERVES OF STEAL

I had to leave town for a couple of days. I was afraid my house would be robbed so I hit on an idea.

①

I left my car in plain sight in the driveway, so crooks would think I'm home.

②

153

BARGAIN HAUNTING

157

LOVE IS A TOO MANY SPLENDORED THING

159

160

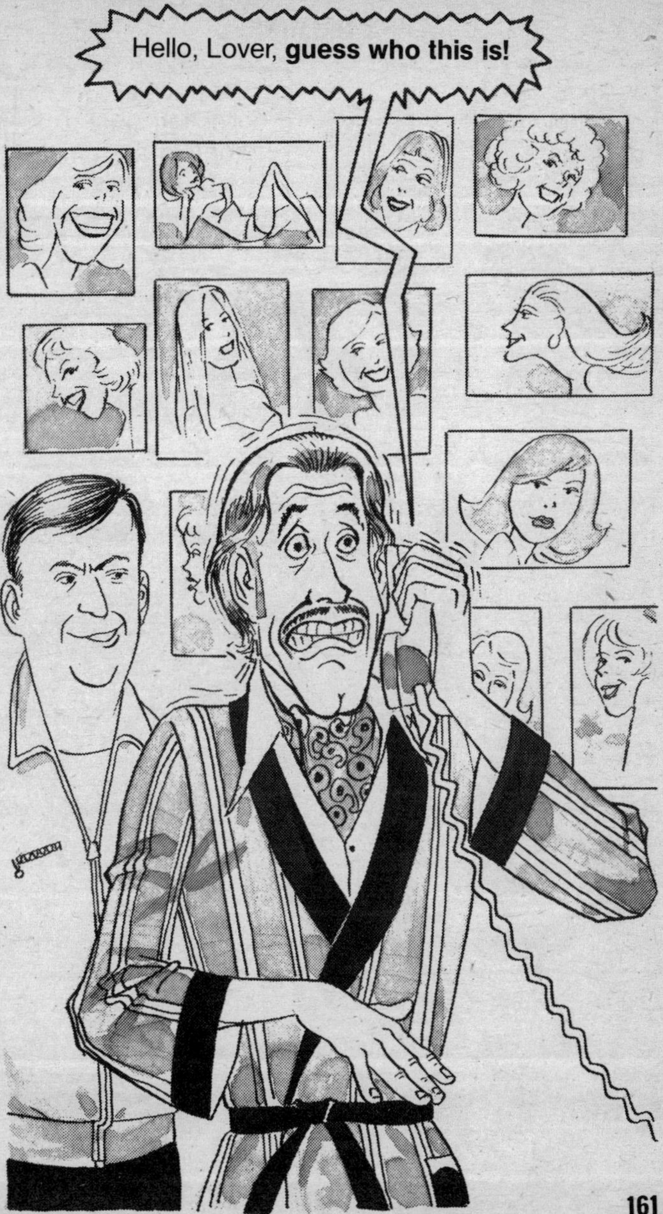
Hello, Lover, **guess who this is!**

GLASS DISMISSED

163

165

167

168

169

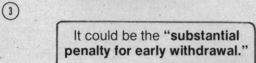

FEELED DAYS

THE BIGGER THEY ARE THE HARDER THEY CRAWL

YOU SEW AND SEW

178

179

GUESSED IN THE HOUSE

181

BUYED YOUR TIME

PARTY IS SUCH SWEET SORROW

185

LETTER ALONE

You've been typing away like crazy. What are you writing?

A letter to the editor.

This is what I said:

Dear Editor,

In these times of turmoil we should all speak up. As in the movie "Network" we should open our windows and shout, "I'm mad as hell and I'm not going to take it anymore."

This is a time for people of courage to stand up and be counted.

Sincerely yours.

187

PHONE NUMB ERRED

I had M.C.I. phone service installed. It cuts the cost of a long distant call in half. So I can call cousin Hilda three thousand miles away very cheaply.

I must get all these numbers correctly. First I dial 742 then 0733—wait for the beep, the 02134, now the area code 718, then 555-6437.

189

CHOW HOUNDED

191